GIFTED & TALENTED®

*To develop
your child's gifts
and talents*

PUZZLES & GAMES

FOR READING AND MATH
BOOK TWO
A Workbook for Ages 4–6

*Reviewed and endorsed by Tiare Hotra, M.Ed.,
Literary and Technology Specialist*

Written by Martha Cheney
Illustrated by Larry Nolte

LOWELL HOUSE JUVENILE

LOS ANGELES

CONTEMPORARY BOOKS

CHICAGO

Requests for such permissions should be addressed to:
Lowell House Juvenile
2020 Avenue of the Stars, Suite 300
Los Angeles, CA 90067

Publisher: Jack Artenstein
Director of Publishing Services: Rena Copperman
Managing Editor, Juvenile Division: Lindsey Hay
Editor in Chief, Juvenile: Amy Downing
Editor: Jessica Oifer
Art Director: Lisa-Theresa Lenthall

Lowell House books can be purchased at special discounts when ordered in bulk for premiums and special sales. Contact Department TC at the above address.

ISBN: 1-56565-566-4

Manufactured in the United States of America

10 9 8 7 6 5 4 3 2

Note to Parents

GIFTED & TALENTED® WORKBOOKS will help develop your child's natural gifts and talents by providing activities to enhance critical and creative thinking skills. These skills of logic and reasoning teach children **how** to think. They are precisely the skills emphasized by teachers of gifted and talented children.

Thinking skills are the skills needed to be able to learn anything at any time. Unlike events, words, and teaching methods, thinking skills never change. If a child has a grasp of how to think, school success and even success in life will become more assured. In addition, the child will become self-confident as he or she approaches new tasks with the ability to think them through and discover solutions.

GIFTED & TALENTED® WORKBOOKS present these skills in a unique way, combining the basic subject areas of reading, language arts, and math with thinking skills. The top of each page is labeled to indicate the specific thinking skill developed. Here are some of the skills you will find.

- Deduction—the ability to reach a logical conclusion by interpreting clues

- Understanding Relationships—the ability to recognize how objects, shapes, and words are similar or dissimilar; to classify or categorize

- Sequencing—the ability to organize events, numbers; to recognize patterns

- Inference—the ability to reach a logical conclusion from given or assumed evidence

- Creative Thinking—the ability to generate unique ideas; to compare and contrast the same elements in different situations; to present imaginative solutions to problems

Each book contains activities that challenge children. The activities range from easier to more difficult. You may need to work with your child on many of the pages, especially with the child who is a non-reader. However, even a non-reader can master thinking skills, and the sooner your child learns how to think, the better. Read the directions to your child and, if necessary, explain them. Let your child choose the activities that interest him or her. When interest wanes, stop. A page or two at a time may be enough, as the child should have fun while learning.

It is important to remember that these activities are designed to teach your child **how to think,** not how to find the right answer. Teachers of gifted children are never surprised when a child discovers a new "right" answer. For example, a child may be asked to choose the object that doesn't belong in this group: a table, a chair, a book, a desk. The best answer is **book,** since all the others are furniture. But a child could respond that all of them belong because they all could be found in an office or a library. The best way to react to this type of response is to praise the child and gently point out that there is another answer, too. While creativity should be encouraged, your child should look for the best and most **suitable** answer.

GIFTED & TALENTED® WORKBOOKS have been written and endorsed by educators. This series will benefit any child who demonstrates curiosity, imagination, a sense of fun and wonder about the world, and a desire to learn. These books will open your child's mind to new experiences and help fulfill his or her true potential.

Draw a picture in each box below. Use the shape that is already in each box as part of your picture. Then write a name for each picture on the line under its box.

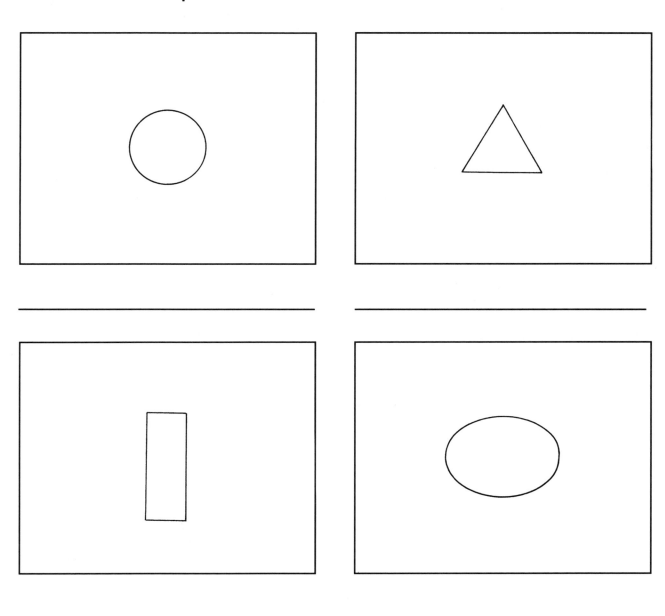

For an extra challenge: On a separate piece of paper, make a list of all the shapes you see.

Draw a picture in each box below. Use the shape that is already in each box as part of your picture. Then write a name for each picture on the line under its box.

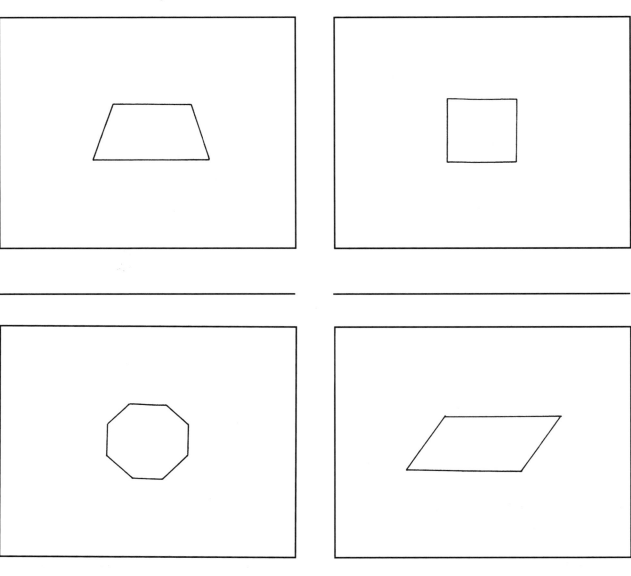

For an extra challenge: On a separate piece of paper, make a list of all the shapes you see. If you don't know the name of a shape, ask an adult to help you.

These playful puppies are hungry. Help the puppies find their bones. Draw a line from each puppy to its own bone.

How many puppies did not find a bone?_____

What do you think might have happened to the missing bone?_____

_____

_____

Badger the Baker has made cookies. Draw a line from each cookie cutter to all the cookies with its same shape.

How many ♡ cookies did Badger make? _____

How many ☆ cookies did Badger make? _____

How many ☾ cookies did Badger make? _____

How many cookies did Badger make altogether? _____

What do you think Badger is going to do with the cookies he made? _____

_____

_____

Samantha found some nuts for her two children. She wants to give each of her children the same number of nuts. There are two different kinds of nuts. Draw a circle around each little squirrel's share of nuts. Make sure each squirrel gets at least one of each kind of nut.

How many nuts does each little squirrel get? _____

Kelly is having a party. She has invited 3 friends. If she and her friends each have 3 cupcakes, how many cupcakes will she need altogether? Draw the cupcakes on the plates to help you find the answer.

Here's an extra challenge! If Kelly puts 2 jelly beans on the top of each cupcake, how many jelly beans will she need altogether? _____

Look at the picture below. Which girl has more toys? Draw a circle around that girl. Which girl has more teddy bears? Draw a square around that girl.

How many of the toys above can roll? _____

Which one of the toys would be the best to play with at the beach? _____

Why? _____

_____

Circle the picture that best answers each question below.

Which animal has more legs?

Which vehicle has more wheels?

Which carton has more eggs?

Which glass has more milk?

Circle the picture that best answers each question below.

Which mother has more ducklings?

Which cowboy has more rope?

Which boy has more freckles?

Which girl has blown a bigger bubble?

Read the directions and then use crayons to color the picture.

Color the small shoes black. Color the large shoes blue. Color the large hat green. Color the small hat red. Color the large pet purple. Color the small pet yellow.

Which pet would you rather have? _____

Why? _____

_____

Connect the dots in order of size. Begin with the smallest dot and end with the largest dot. Make sure you draw straight lines. Use a ruler if you need help. When you are finished, connect the smallest dot to the largest dot.

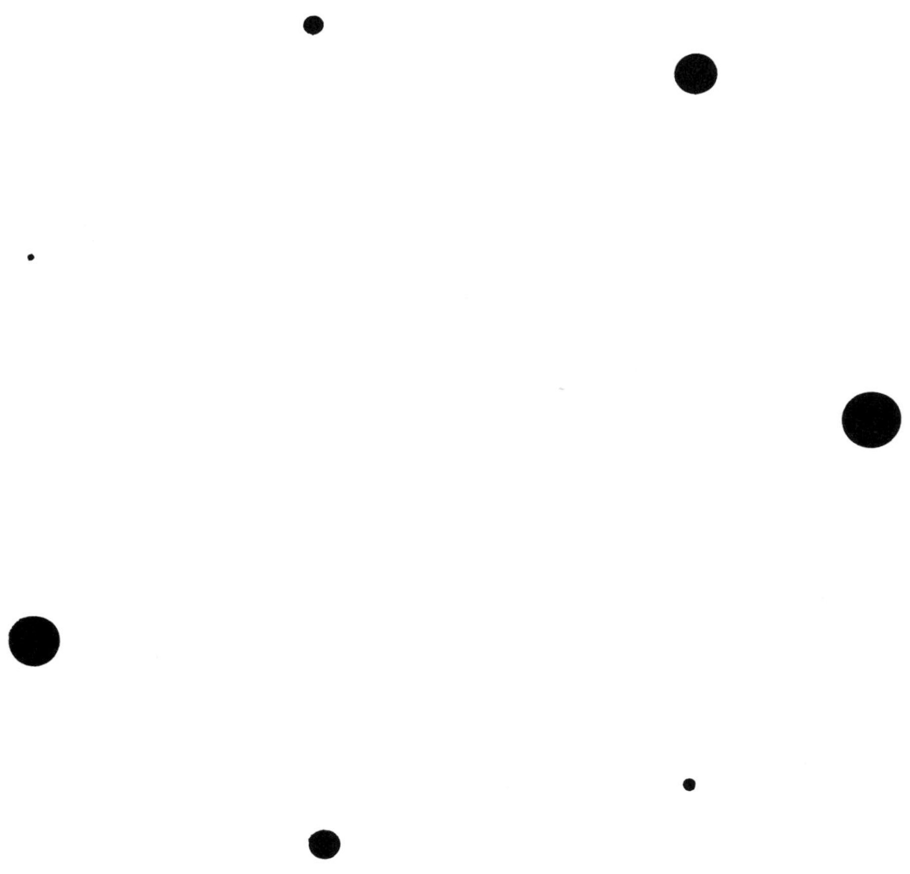

What shape did you make? _____

Now use a different color to connect the dots from largest to smallest.

Did you make the same shape? _____

Look at the ships and boats in the picture below. They are all made from these six shapes: △, □, ▭, ○, ◡, ⬭. Count how many there are of each shape in the picture. Color one square on the graph for each shape you count.

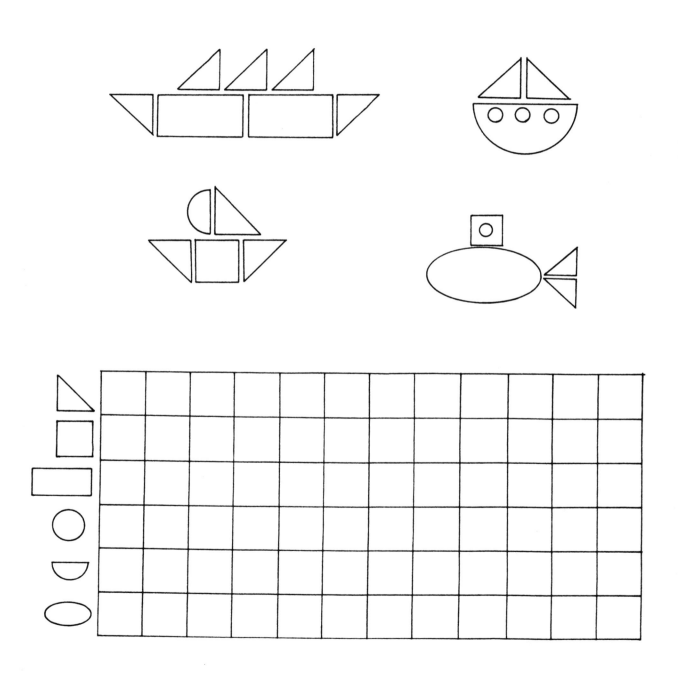

Look at each row of shapes. Draw an **X** on the one shape that does not belong in each row. Then tell why that shape does not belong.

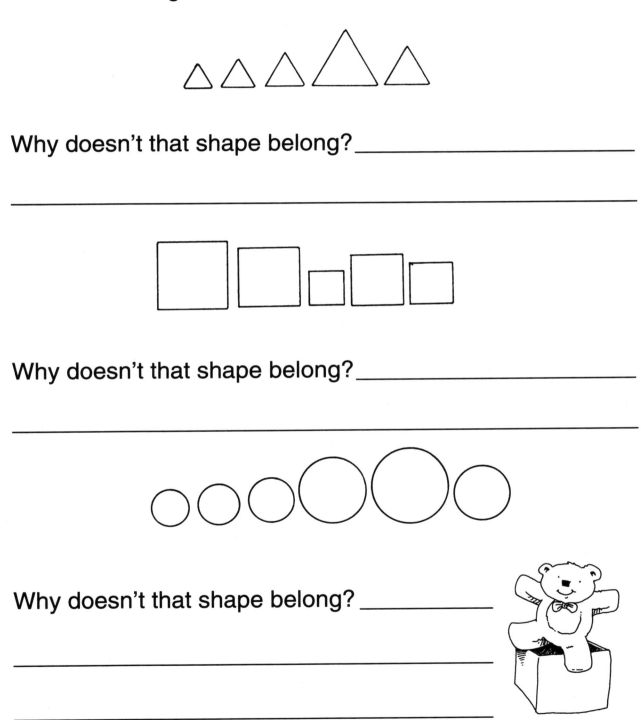

Why doesn't that shape belong?_____

_____

Why doesn't that shape belong?_____

_____

Why doesn't that shape belong? _____

_____

_____

Look at each row of shapes. Draw an **X** on the one shape that does not belong in each row. Then tell why that shape does not belong.

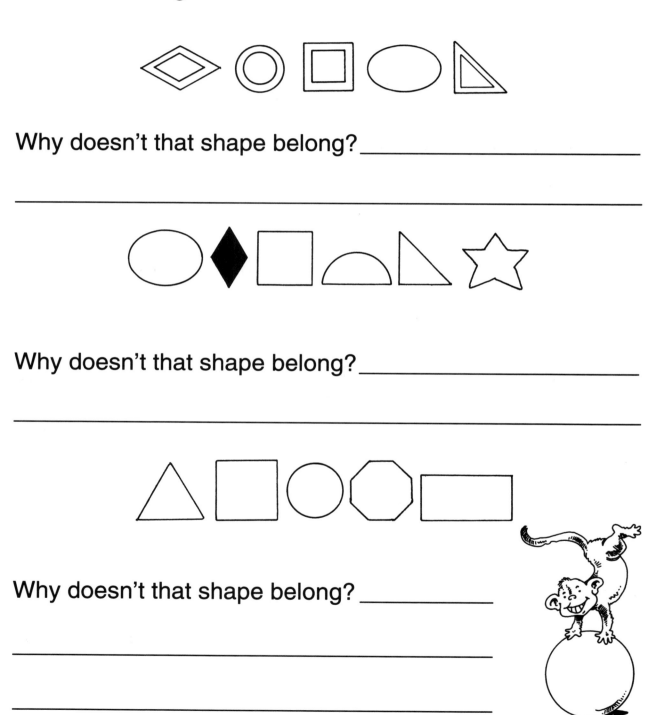

Why doesn't that shape belong? _____

_____

Why doesn't that shape belong? _____

_____

Why doesn't that shape belong? _____

_____

_____

Look at each row of shapes. Draw an **X** on the one shape that does not belong in each row. Then tell why that shape does not belong.

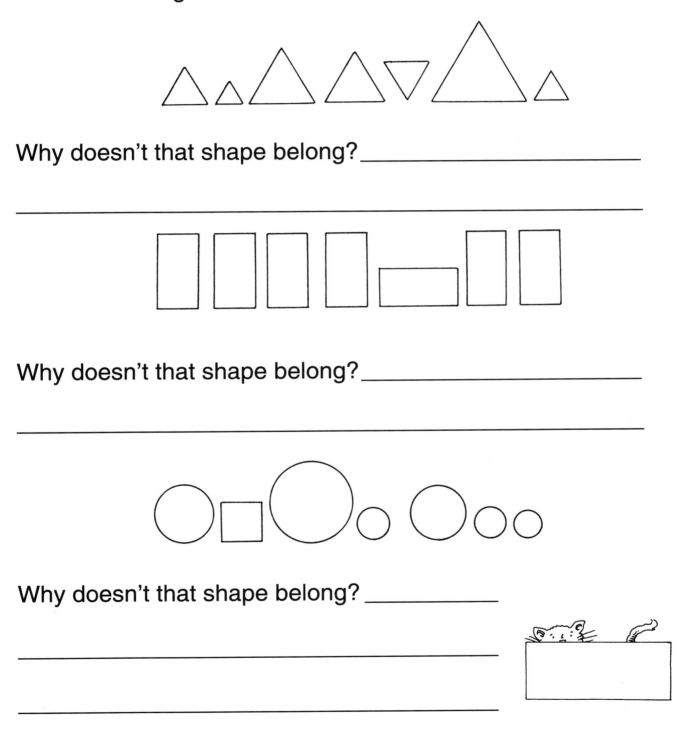

Why doesn't that shape belong? _____

_____

Why doesn't that shape belong? _____

_____

Why doesn't that shape belong? _____

_____

_____

Complete each ice-cream cone by drawing the number of scoops written on the cone. Use crayons to make each scoop a different color. Draw a cherry on top of the ice-cream cone with more scoops of ice cream.

What flavor is each ice-cream scoop that you drew?

_____

_____

Which is your favorite flavor?_____

Use crayons to color each flower in the basket. Use the colors red, yellow, blue, and pink. Color the flowers so that no flowers that are the same color touch each other.

How many passengers are in each car of the circus train?
The passengers can be people or animals. Write the
number of passengers in the box at the top of each car. Use
a red crayon to color the car with the most passengers.
Use a blue crayon to color the car with the least passengers.

Including the engineers, how many passengers does the train have altogether? _____

Benny's mother asked him to pick 6 apples from the apple tree so she could make an apple pie. Help Benny find his way through the maze to the tree that has the correct number of apples.

Practice counting by fives. The pictures in each row will help you. Fill in the blank next to each row to show how many fingers or toes there are in each one.

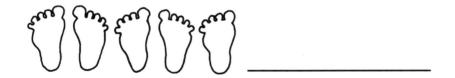

Extra challenges! How many fingers and toes are there altogether? _____

Now count by fives as high as you can. Can you go all the way to 100? _____

Practice counting by tens. The pictures in each row will help you. Fill in the blank next to each picture to show how many space creatures there are in each row.

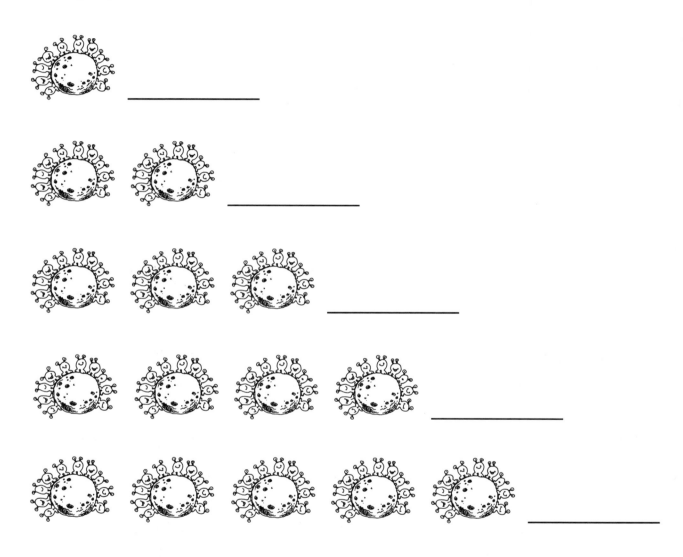

Extra challenges! How many space creatures are there altogether? _____

Now count by tens as high as you can. Can you go all the way to 1000? _____

Sally is shopping for some items she needs to do her work. She has 3 dimes, 4 nickels, and 4 pennies to spend.

Which item could Sally buy with **exactly** 2 dimes and 1 nickel? Use a crayon to color that item blue.

Which item could Sally buy with **exactly** 3 nickels and 1 penny? Use a crayon to color that item red.

Which item could Sally buy with **exactly** 1 dime and 3 pennies? Use a crayon to color that item yellow.

Draw an **X** on the item that Sally does not have enough money to buy.

What is Sally's work? _____

Read the time shown on each clock below. Draw a picture
in each box that shows what you usually do at that time
of day.

in the morning (A.M.)

noon

at night (P.M.)

Draw a circle around each clock or watch that reads
8 o'clock.

For an extra challenge: Near each watch or clock, write
the time that it shows. Use your favorite color crayon to
color the clock or watch that is closest to the time that it is
right now.

Look at the spots on each ladybug's right wing. Then draw spots on each left wing so that every ladybug has a total of 4 spots. **Hint:** One ladybug might not need any more spots!

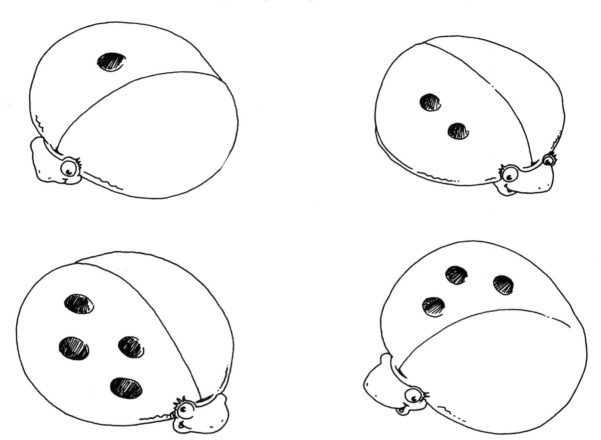

How many spots are there on all of the ladybugs combined? _____

For an extra challenge: Draw 6 legs and 2 antennae on each ladybug.
How many legs are there on all of the ladybugs combined? _____
How many antennae are there on all of the ladybugs combined? _____

The children who went to Antonia's Valentine's Day party each received a balloon. Some of the balloons were red and some were pink. Answer the questions that follow.
Hint: Coloring the pictures will help you.

If 4 children chose red balloons, how many chose pink ones? _____

If 3 children chose pink balloons, how many chose red ones? _____

If 5 children chose pink balloons, how many chose red ones? _____

Draw your own Valentine's Day card below.

In autumn, the leaves of many trees change colors. Follow the directions to color the leaves on the rows of trees below. Use only two crayon colors: red and yellow. Be sure to color all the trees in each row.

Color the leaves on 2 trees red. How many trees will have yellow leaves? _____ Now color those leaves.

Color the leaves on 1 tree red. How many trees will have yellow leaves? _____ Now color those leaves.

Color the leaves on 3 trees red. How many trees will have yellow leaves? _____ Now color those leaves.

Look at this stack of blocks. How many blocks are in the stack?_____ Draw more blocks on top of the stack until you have made a stack of 7 blocks. How many blocks did you add? _____

Look at this stack of blocks. How many blocks are in the stack?_____ Draw more blocks on top of the stack until you have made a stack of 7 blocks. How many blocks did you add? _____

How many blocks do the children have altogether? _____

For an extra challenge: On a separate piece of paper, draw a picture of a structure you could build using exactly that many blocks.

The spiders are all dressed up to go to a party. They even have their dancing shoes on. Look carefully at their shoes. Then answer the questions below each picture.

How many shoes have bows? _____
How many shoes have buckles? _____

How many shoes have bows? _____
How many shoes have buckles? _____

How many shoes have bows? _____
How many shoes have buckles? _____

How many shoes have bows? _____
How many shoes have buckles? _____

Now tell a story about the spiders' party.

Julie is making daisy chains. She is using purple daisies and yellow daisies. Use crayons to color each chain so that a **different** number of purple daisies is used each time!

Look at **all** of the daisy chains together.

How many daisies did you color purple? _____

How many daisies did you color yellow? _____

For an extra challenge: If Julie put all of her daisy chains together into one chain, how many inches long would the chain be? **Hint:** Ask a parent if you need help.

Look at the pictures in the boxes on these two pages. Circle the pictures that go together to tell a story. Then number the pictures in an order that makes sense. When you're finished, tell a story using the pictures as a guide.

_____

_____

_____

_____

_____

_____

_____

_____

Use the clues below to find the magical mushroom. Then circle the magical mushroom.

The magical mushroom has 3 spots.
The magical mushroom is near 2 flowers.
The magical mushroom is tall.

For an extra challenge: Tell a story to a friend or a family member about the magical mushroom.

Kyle's picture won first place in the school art show. Use the clues to figure out which picture is Kyle's. Color his picture with crayons.

Kyle's picture is square.
Kyle's picture has a tree in it.
Kyle's picture is large.
Kyle's picture does not have a frame.

Think of a name for Kyle's picture. Write it here.

Mallory likes to feed the ducks at the park. One duck is her favorite. Use the clues to figure out which one. Then circle that duck.

It has a ring around its neck.
It has curly tail feathers.
It is not white.
It does not have spots on its back.

Why do you think Mallory likes this duck the best? _____

_____

Look at the pictures on this page. Each picture has a word below it. Use crayons to color the pictures that have the correct label below them.

cap

hat

man

sun

rat

bus

cat

Draw an **X** over the word beneath each picture that is labeled incorrectly. Then write a new label for those pictures.

To play this game, you will need 24 1" × 1" squares of construction paper and a partner. Ask an adult to help you cut out the squares. You can use any color paper you want.

Place one square over each box on these two pages. Make sure the number or picture in each box is covered completely.

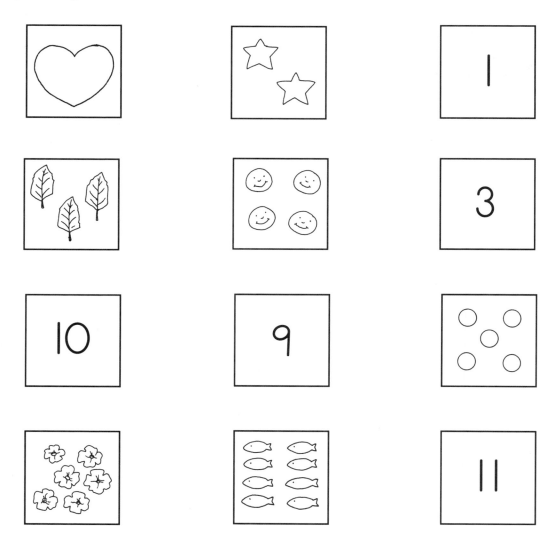

Take turns with your partner removing two squares of paper at a time. If the two boxes you uncover go together, keep the two pieces of paper. If they do not go together, put the papers back over the boxes. Continue to play until all the papers have been removed. The person with the most squares of paper at the end of the game wins.

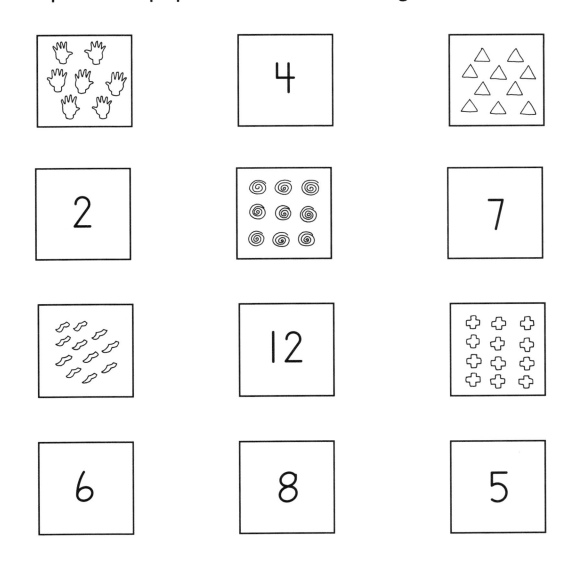

Circle each word that tells something about the picture below. Then explain to a friend or a family member why you chose those words.

one   good   sad   rug   big   run

Make a list of other words that tell something about the picture.

_____   _____

_____   _____

_____   _____

_____   _____

_____   _____

Circle each word that tells something about the picture below. Explain to a friend or a family member why you chose those words.

go   red   two   cat   boy   eat

Make up a story about the picture. Write it below, or tell the story to a parent and ask him or her to write it for you.

_____

_____

_____

_____

_____

_____

Circle each word that tells something about the picture below. Explain to a friend or a family member why you chose those words.

man   in   bear   bag   box   little   big

Write the words you did not choose on the line below.

_____

Then draw a picture in the box that illustrates those words.

Circle each word that tells something about the picture below. Explain to a friend or a family member why you chose those words.

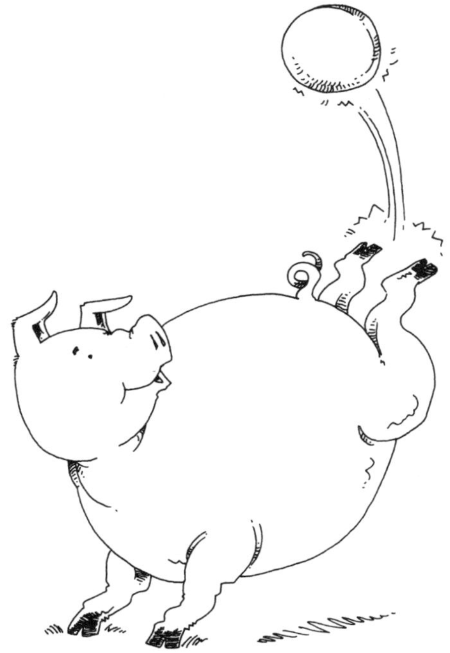

pig   bat   ball   up   hit   down

Make up a story about the picture. Write it below, or tell the story to a parent and ask him or her to write it for you.

_____

_____

_____

_____

_____

_____

Fill in the blanks in the sentences below. Use a different word in each sentence. Make sure each word you choose makes sense in the sentence. Draw a picture in the box to illustrate the sentence you like best.

Peter went to the _____ to get some water.

Peter went to the _____ to get some water.

Peter went to the _____ to get some water.

Fill in the blanks in the sentences below. Use a different word in each sentence. Make sure each word you choose makes sense in the sentence. Draw a picture in the box to illustrate the sentence you like best.

Jaime went for a walk on a _____ day.

Jaime went for a walk on a _____ day.

Jaime went for a walk on a _____ day.

Fill in the blanks in the sentences below. Use a different word in each sentence. Make sure each word you choose makes sense in the sentence. Draw a picture to illustrate the sentence you like best.

Serena found a _____ at the beach.

Serena found a _____ at the beach.

Serena found a _____ at the beach.

Draw a circle around each animal described by all three clues below.

I could fit in a teacup.
I am a pet.
I like to be wet.

How many animals did you circle? _____
Explain your choices to a friend or a family member.

Which one of your choices best fits all the clues? Why?

_____

_____

Draw a circle around each animal described by all three clues below.

I am bigger than a football.
I do not have any hair.
I have sharp teeth.

How many animals did you circle? _____
Explain your choices to a friend or a family member.

Which one of your choices best fits all the clues? Why?

_____

_____

Look at the pictures in the grid below. Each row (across or down) contains three objects that belong together in some way. Fill in each blank with a word that describes how the objects in each row are related.

	Things that you _____	Things that are _____	Things that are _____
Things that are _____			
Things that are _____			
Things that are _____			

Look at the pictures in the grid below. Each row (across or down) contains three objects that belong together in some way. Fill in each blank with a word that describes how the objects in each row are related.

	Things that you _____	Things that are _____	Things that you _____
Things that are _____			
Things that are _____			
Things that are _____			

Look at the letters floating in Allison's bowl of soup. How many words can you spell using those letters? You may use each letter more than once.

Write your words here. _____

_____

How many words did you write? _____

Make up a story using some of your words. Tell your story to a friend or a family member.

Look at the letters on the leaves of this tree. How many words can you spell using those letters? You may use each letter more than once.

Write your words here. _____

_____

How many words did you write? _____

Make up a story using some of your words. Tell your story to a friend or a family member.

Look at the letters on the chocolates in this box. How many words can you spell using those letters? You may use each letter more than once.

Write your words here. _____

_____

How many words did you write? _____

Make up a story using some of your words. Tell your story to a friend or a family member.

Hank, Frank, and Spanky are the horses that live at the Big Sky Ranch. Use the clues below to find out each horse's name. Write the correct name near each horse's picture.

Hank has a long tail and spots.
Frank has spots and a short tail.
Spanky has a short tail but no spots.

_____   _____

                              _____

If you were to visit the Big Sky Ranch, which horse would you most like to ride? _____

Why? _____

Use the clues below to find out which cowgirl is which.
Write each cowgirl's name near her picture.

Vanessa wears boots with pointed toes. She wears a white hat and a striped shirt.

Amy wears boots with round toes. She wears a white hat and a flowered shirt.

Clara wears boots with pointed toes. She wears a black hat and a striped shirt.

_____   _____

_____

What chores do you think the cowgirls are getting ready to do? _____

_____

Answers

Page 5
Answers will vary.
Extra challenge: circle, triangle, rectangle, oval

Page 6
Answers will vary.
Extra challenge: trapezoid, square, octagon, parallelogram

Page 7
Answers will vary. One possible answer is:

1 puppy

Answers will vary. Possible answers include: It is in the hole, behind the tree stump, or under the rock.

Page 8

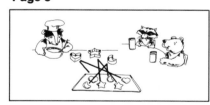

2 ♡ cookies

2 ☆ cookies

2 ☾ cookies

6 cookies altogether
Answers will vary. One possible answer: He is going to share them with his friends.

Page 9
Parent: Child should circle 2 groups of 4 nuts. Each group should include at least 1 of each kind of nut. Each squirrel gets 4 nuts.

Page 10
12 cupcakes
Extra challenge: 24 jelly beans

Page 11

Four toys can roll: 2 trucks, 1 car, and 1 ball.
The boat or the ball might be best to play with at the beach. *Parent:* Accept variant answers, but ask child to explain his or her response.

Pages 12–13

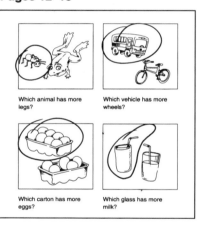

Page 14
Parent: Make sure child colors picture according to directions. Rest of answer will vary.

Page 15

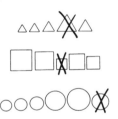

A star.
Yes.

Page 16

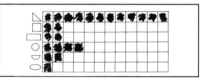

Page 17

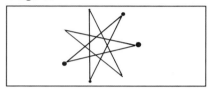

These shapes do not belong because they are out of size order.

Page 18

It doesn't have a smaller shape inside the larger.

It is the only shape that is filled in completely.

It is the only shape that is circular.

Page 19

It is the only triangle standing on its point.

It is the only rectangle lying horizontally.

It is the only square in a row of circles.

Page 20

Parent: Make sure child draws correct number of scoops on the cones. Child should draw a cherry on the cone with 5 scoops.
Rest of answer will vary.

Page 21

Answers will vary. *Parent:* Check to see that no flowers that touch each other are the same color.

Pages 22–23

The monkey car has the most passengers and should be colored red. The elephant car has the least and should be colored blue. There are 13 passengers altogether.

Page 24

Page 25

5 fingers
10 toes
15 fingers
20 toes
25 toes
There are 75 fingers and toes altogether.
Rest of answer will vary.

Page 26

10 space creatures
20 space creatures
30 space creatures
40 space creatures
50 space creatures
There are 150 space creatures altogether.
Rest of answer will vary.

Page 27

Sally could buy the paintbrush with 2 dimes and 1 nickel.
She could buy the eraser with 3 nickels and 1 penny.
She could buy the pencil with 1 dime and 3 pennies.
She does not have enough money to buy the art paper.
Sally is an artist.

Page 28

Answers will vary. *Parent:* Make sure child's drawing makes sense for each time of day.

Page 29

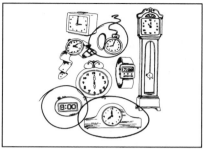

Extra challenge: *Parent*—Make sure child colors the correct clock or watch.

Page 30

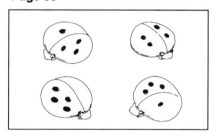

16 spots
24 legs
8 antennae

Page 31

1, 2, 0
Rest of answer will vary.

Page 32

4, 5, 3

Page 33

Parent: Child should add 3 blocks to the left stack and 5 blocks to the right stack. There are 14 blocks altogether.
Extra challenge: *Parent*—Child's drawing should contain 14 blocks.
Rest of answer will vary.

Page 34

2 bows and 6 buckles
5 bows and 3 buckles
4 bows and 4 buckles
7 bows and 1 buckle
Rest of answer will vary.

Page 35
Answers will vary. *Parent:* Make sure that a different number of daisies is purple on each chain. Rest of answer will vary.
Extra challenge: *Parent*—Discuss child's answer to determine how he or she reached the estimate.

Pages 36–37

Page 38

Extra challenge: Rest of answer will vary.

Page 39
Kyle's picture has a boy flying his kite with his dog.
Rest of answer will vary.

Page 40

Rest of answer will vary.

Page 41
Parent: Child should color the hat, sun, man, bus, and cat. The car and dog are labeled incorrectly.
Their labels should be X'd out and rewritten by the child.

Pages 42–43
Parent: As child plays the game, make sure that child understands the relationship between the number and the picture of a number group.

Page 44
Answers will vary.
Possible answers include:
There is **one** mouse. He is sitting on a **rug**. The cheese is **good**. The rug is **big**. Rest of answer will vary.

Page 45
Answers will vary.
Possible answers include:
There are **two** children. One is a **boy**. They want to **go** across the street. The light is **red**.
Rest of answer will vary.

Page 46
Answers will vary.
Possible answers include:
The **man** has a **big box**. There is a **bear in** the box.
Rest of answer will vary.

Page 47
Answers will vary.
Possible answers include:
The **pig** is playing with the **ball**. He likes to **hit** it **up** in the air.
Rest of answer will vary.

Page 48
Answers will vary. Possible answers include: refrigerator, sink, well, stream, kitchen

Page 49
Answers will vary. Possible answers include: rainy, windy, snowy, sunny, beautiful, stormy, school

Page 50
Answers will vary. Possible answers include: shell, starfish, quarter, towel, bucket, crab

Page 51
Answers will vary but should include fish, frog, and earthworm. Fish is probably the best answer, but allow variant answers and ask child to explain his or her reasoning.

Page 52
Answers will vary but should include alligator and shark. Either of these might be seen as the best answer. Ask child to explain his or her reasoning.

Page 53

	Things that you **drink**	Things that are **cold**	Things that are **soft**
Things that are **wet**			
Things that are **sweet**			
Things that are **white**			

Page 54

Page 55

Answers will vary. Possible answers include: man, pan, pat, pot, top, ton, ant, hop, oat

Page 56

Answers will vary. Possible answers include: rat, rag, bag, bit, fit, fig, tag, tar, tab, gift

Page 57

Answers will vary. Possible answers include: lid, hid, side, hide, wide, den, wish, dish, led

Page 58

Rest of answer will vary.

Page 59

Rest of answer will vary.

Other

books that will help develop your child's gifts and talents

Workbooks:
- Reading (4–6) $4.95
- Math (4–6) $4.95
- Language Arts (4–6) $4.95
- Puzzles & Games for Reading and Math (4–6) $3.95
- Puzzles & Games for Reading and Math Book Two (4–6) $4.95
- Puzzles & Games for Critical and Creative Thinking (4–6) $4.95
- Reading Book Two (4–6) $4.95
- Math Book Two (4–6) $4.95
- Phonics (4–6) $4.95
- Phonics Puzzles & Games (4–6) $4.95
- Math Puzzles & Games (4–6) $4.95
- Reading Puzzles & Games (4–6) $4.95
- Math (6–8) $3.95
- Language Arts (6–8) $4.95
- Puzzles & Games for Reading and Math (6–8) $3.95
- Puzzles & Games for Critical and Creative Thinking (6–8) $3.95
- Puzzles & Games for Reading and Math, Book Two (6–8) $3.95
- Phonics (6–8) $4.95
- Reading Comprehension (6–8) $4.95

Reference Workbooks:
- Word Book (4–6) $3.95
- Almanac (6–8) $3.95
- Atlas (6–8) $3.95
- Dictionary (6–8) $3.95

Story Starters:
- My First Stories (6–8) $3.95
- Stories About Me (6–8) $3.95
- Stories About Animals (6–8) $4.95

Question & Answer Books:
- The Gifted & Talented® Question & Answer Book for Ages 4–6 $5.95
- The Gifted & Talented® Question & Answer Book for Ages 6–8 $5.95
- Gifted & Talented® More Questions & Answers for Ages 4–6 $5.95
- Gifted & Talented® More Questions & Answers for Ages 6–8 $5.95

Drawing Books:
- Learn to Draw (6 and up) $5.95

Readers:
- Double the Trouble (6–8) $7.95
- Time for Bed (6–8) $7.95

For Parents:
- How to Develop Your Child's Gifts and Talents During the Elementary Years $11.95
- How to Develop Your Child's Gifts and Talents in Math $15.00
- How to Develop Your Child's Gifts and Talents in Reading $15.00
- How to Develop Your Child's Gifts and Talents in Vocabulary $15.00

Available where good books are sold! **or** *Send a check or money order, plus shipping charges, to:*

Handy Worksheet

Department TC
Lowell House
2020 Century Park East, Suite 300
Los Angeles, CA 90067

For special or bulk sales, call (800) 552-7551, EXT 30

Note: Minimum order of three titles. **On a separate piece of paper,**
please specify exact titles and ages and include a breakdown of costs, as follows:

(# of books) _____	x $3.95	=	_____
(# of books) _____	x $4.95	=	_____
(# of books) _____	x $5.95	=	_____
(# of books) _____	x $7.95	=	_____
(# of books) _____	x $11.95	=	_____
(# of books) _____	x $15.00	=	_____

(Subtotal)	=	_____
California residents add 8.25% sales tax	=	_____
Shipping charges (# of books) _____ x $1.00/ book	=	_____
Total cost	=	_____